SONIC & FRIENDS

STICKER ACTIVITY BOOK

by Karl Jones

PENGUIN YOUNG READERS LICENSES
An Imprint of Penguin Random House LLC, New York

Visit us online at www.penguinrandomhouse.com.

ISBN 9780593093023   10 9 8 7

Ready, Set, Go!

Sonic, Shadow, and Silver are racing to claim a Chaos Emerald. Follow the lines to see who won.

Green Hill Maze

Sonic and his friends can't figure out which way is up and which way is down. Help them find their way through the maze to catch Dr. Eggman before he escapes.

Coloring Mishmash

Dr. Eggman created a machine that removed all the color from the Green Hill. Can you save the day by coloring in the heroes before it's too late?

Wacky Word Search

Sonic is the fastest, bravest hedgehog around, but he can't do everything on his own. Help Sonic find his friends listed below in the wacky word search on the next page!

AMY

KNUCKLES

BLAZE

BIG

ROUGE

CREAM

CHEESE

SILVER

CHAO

VECTOR

L K A C G E L K A E I A I B
R N K H U D O L C E L V V B
Y U N A B C K M H C R R R I
A C I E O R R S A C C G E G
V K C K C I L E O S E B V K
D L S S L I A T A I Z A L V
M E C T R I O A B M A A I E
M S H R O U G E C S L K S C
E O E N A G B R A N B R R T
C E E U N A O C E L E E E O
R C S E S R B C D C L S D R
M D E D A U M P L N L K S E
C K I M R S O N I C U S K H
I K Y N A C G F E R D B D A

Sonic & Dr. Eggman Showdown

Sonic has finally caught up with the evil Dr. Eggman. Help finish the story of their battle below!

Sonic runs at Dr. Eggman and yells

_____

_____

_____

Dr. Eggman is sneaky. He tries to stop Sonic with one of his robotic

_____

_____

But Sonic is too fast. He races around Dr. Eggman until the bad guy _____

_____

Sonic has won again, but Dr. Eggman has escaped and _____

_____

_____!

On this page, complete the comic strips below to show all the awesome action described in the epic battle you've written!

Heroic Word Scramble

Someone has scrambled up the letters in these names. Help unscramble them so these heroes can join the fight!

CNLKUSEK

_ _ _ _ _ _ _ _ _

RESVLI

_ _ _ _ _ _

CTVERO

_ _ _ _ _ _

There's no time to rest now! Draw all the awesome heroes helping Sonic battle Dr. Eggman and chase him out of the Green Hill!

Sky Sanctuary Battle

Dr. Eggman secretly sent his robots to attack the Sky Sanctuary. Knuckles needs help protecting his home island. Use stickers from the back of this book to create an army of heroes and defend this sacred area.

Destroying the Chemical Plant

Sonic and his friends have finally caught up to Dr. Eggman. They need your help in describing this epic battle to save the world from Dr. Eggman.

Sonic rushes toward Dr. Eggman and

_____

_____

Tails destroys one of the Badniks by

building a _____

_____

Amy runs to Sonic's side and _____

_____

_____

Knuckles helps Sonic stop Dr. Eggman.

Together the two heroes _____

_____

A defeated Dr. Eggman sneaks away

to _____

_____ .

On this page, draw the epic battle you've described and send Dr. Eggman packing!

PAGE 2

SONIC WINS!

PAGE 3

PAGE 7

```
L K A C G E L K A E I A I B
R N K H U D O L C E L V V B
Y U N A B C K M H C R R R I
A C I E O R R S A C C G E G
V K C K C I L E O S E B V K
D L S S L I A T A I Z A L V
M E C T R I O A B M A A I E
M S H R O U G E C S L K S C
E O E N A G B R A N B R R T
C E E U N A O C E L E E E O
R C S E S R B C D C L S D R
M D E D A U M P L N L K S E
C K I M R S O N I C U S K H
I K Y N A C G F E R D B D A
```

PAGE 10

CNLKUSEK
<u>KNUCKLES</u>

RESVLI
<u>SILVER</u>

CTVERO
<u>VECTOR</u>

©SEGA

©SEGA